Australia has many animals that live in the water. Crabs live in the sea under rocks. Crabs would have been good food for the First People.

In the rivers there were big fish to eat. The First People used fish traps and spears to catch cod.

Eels were a food for the First People. Eels live in rivers and bays on the coast. Eels were trapped. Eels were cooked for food.

In the bays and coast there were many fish. Fish were caught in traps or by spear. The First People caught fish in canoes.

A trap was made from reeds. Fish would go into the trap looking for food. The fish could not find the hole to get out.

Oysters are called shellfish. There were many types of shellfish that could be food. The First People collected shellfish. Large hills of shells were left by the First People.

In the warm waters of Australia there were turtles. The First People used turtles for food. Turtles were hunted in canoes.

Dugongs lived in the warm waters of Australia. The First People hunted the dugongs for food. A dugong could feed a lot of people.

Crocodiles were very dangerous.
Crocodiles will attack people.
The First People were afraid of crocodiles.

Sharks were in all waters close to shore. Some sharks were small and were food for the First People. Large sharks could be very dangerous.

Whales were seen by the First People. Whales swam along the coast going to the warm waters off Australia. Baby whales were born in the warm waters.

Word bank

dugong
eels
Australia
animals
spear
oysters
turtle
people
crocodile
sharks
whales
trapped
cooked
canoes
caught
looking
shellfish
hunted
dangerous
afraid